Cloé Fontaine

My Japanese Sketchbook

Flammarion

Translated from the French by *Susan Schneider*
Copyediting: *Kate Lancaster*
Typesetting: *Claude-Olivier Four*
Proofreading: *Chrisoula Petridis*
Color separation: *Eurésys*

Previously published in French as *Mes Carnets du Japon* © Éditions Flammarion, 2002
English-language edition © Éditions Flammarion, 2004

Haiku:
© 1979, *Japanese Linked Poetry,* Princeton University Press.
© 1910, *Japanese Poetry,* John Murray.
© 1996, *The Haiku Seasons—Poetry of the Natural World,* Kodansha International.
© 1998, *Traces of Dreams: Landscape, Cultural Memory and the Poetry of Bashó,* Stanford University Press.
© 1973, *A History of Haiku volume I,* The Hokuseido Press.

Watercolors:
© Cloé Fontaine
© Flammarion, Paris, June 2002

26, rue Racine
75006 Paris
France

www.editions.flammarion.com

04 05 06 4 3 2 1

FC0434-04-III
ISBN: 2-0803-0434-8
Dépôt légal: 03/2004

My Japanese Sketchbook was published with the support of:

S.A Tricots Saint-James
B.P. 1 - 50240 Saint-James
France
www.saint-james-tricots.com

Printed in Spain by JCG

開運招福
京都北山
金閣舎利殿御守護
家内安全
鹿苑禪寺

My Japanese Sketchbook

Cloé Fontaine

Preface by Ryoichi Shigeta

Flammarion

Preface by Ryoichi Shigeta

Cloé Fontaine, a young French architect with a passion for color, was introduced to us by our friend Jean-Philippe Lenclos, a designer-colorist. After a long trip through Eurasia, she arrived in Tokyo and spent a few days in Kyoto before coming to discover the island of Shikoku. She was to stay with Tamako and me in our countryside home, typically Japanese in style and surrounded by rice paddies.

Cloé enchanted me with her Moroccan sketchbook. Her palette of colors and the concise nature of her drawings give her watercolors a soothing sense of tenderness and solace. Her use of chiaroscuro forms sharp, simple contrasts of soft hues, and her own distinctive range of colors conjures up a sense of limpidity.

With the eye of a young architect, attentive to nature and detail, Cloé has coined the term "archi-texture," allowing us to reach deeply into the intimate world of material.

Cloé found great sagacity in the Japanese landscape—which brings to mind our pilgrimage to the temple of Kompira-san, dedicated to the guardian deity of the sea and seafarers. In oppressive heat and humidity, we climbed the eight hundred steps together, following an ever-changing path, now narrow and hemmed in, then wide, steep, lingering, sometimes tree-covered and sometimes open to the skies. There was emotion in the air that day with Cloé—I thought about our ancestors, I sensed the freshness of her project, the day was beautiful and warm.

Her fascination with old objects and fabrics let her play with the pictorial palettes of my country—so varied, vivid, picturesque, and sometimes even bizarre—found in everyday life, the world of theater, and traditional costumes. However, even today the true colors of Japan are still black and white, synonymous with ceremony and mourning, and red and white, the colors of festivals and celebrations.

I was delighted to find that a young French architect would express her travel impressions through sketches, and above all through color. When I think of Cloé, I travel to Kompira-san, and it is beautiful and warm—just like in her watercolors.

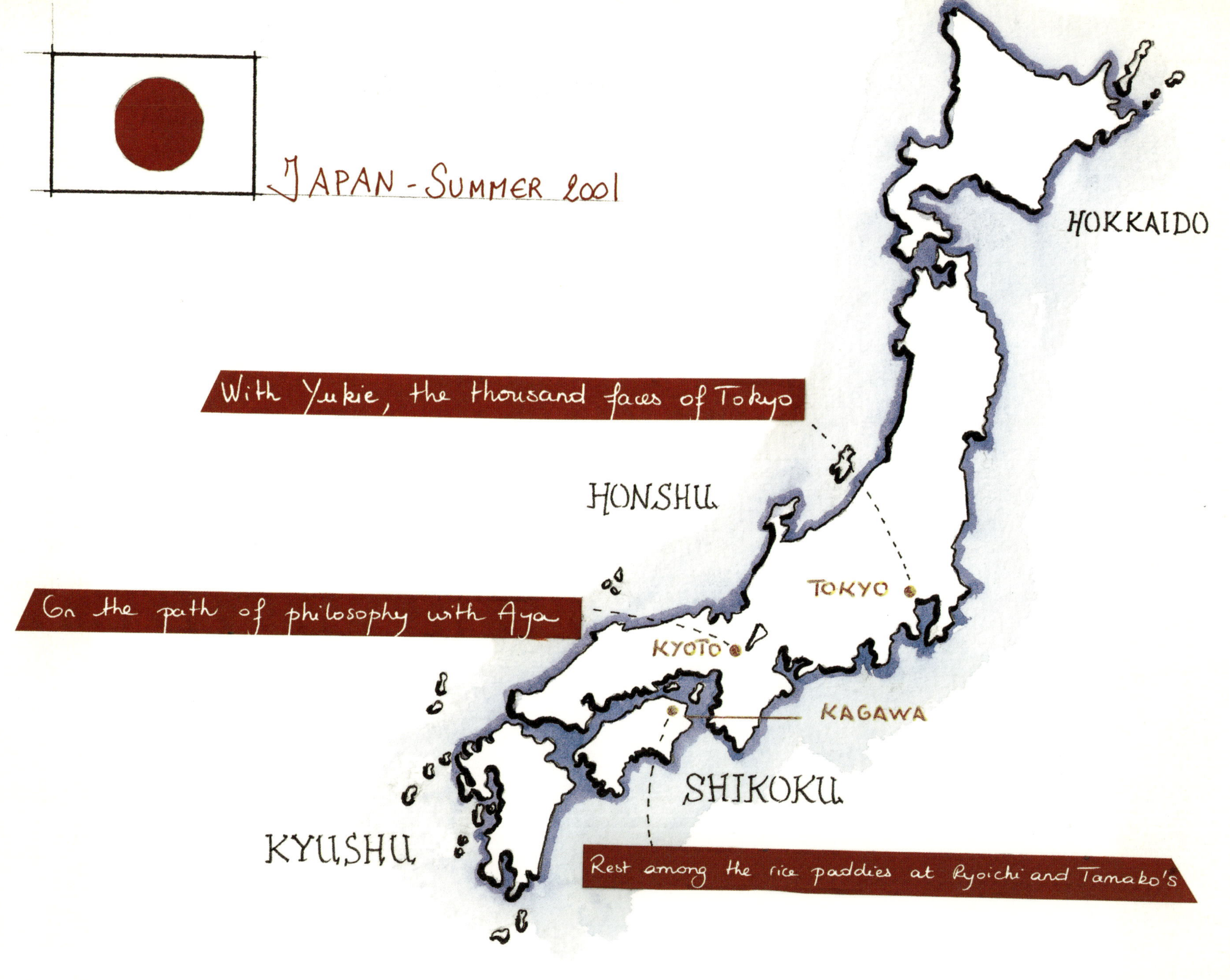

JAPAN - SUMMER 2001
HOKKAIDO
With Yukie, the thousand faces of Tokyo
HONSHU
TOKYO
On the path of philosophy with Aya
KYOTO
KAGAWA
SHIKOKU
KYUSHU
Rest among the rice paddies at Ryoichi and Tamako's

Contents

平静

With the passing time...
Between passion and reason,
To my parents.

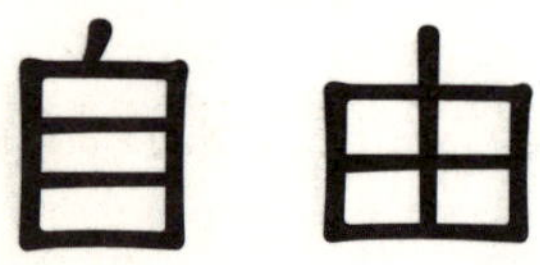

Secrets beneath parasols,
Far from Aragon, in Castilla y Leon,
To Ben and his fair Belen.

Secrets beneath parasols,
Far from Aragon, in Castilla y Leon,
To Ben and his fair Belen.

Entering Japan, as if enclosed within a bubble… I am floating above an unknown land, delicate and fragrant—so soothing after my chaotic journey through Siberia and Mongolia.

For me, the teeming city of Tokyo is a haven of peace; strangely, it evokes similar sensations to those experienced in the heart of the Mongolian plains! So strange is this new life in the land of the Rising Sun—where I imagined noise, crowds, speed, and stress I find silence, serenity, slowness, and a new contentment.

In geisha country, I let my gaze linger over the colors of the architecture and its archi-texture, over the customs and costumes, the landscapes of this wise land, and the modernity of its modern cities. In the course of these four chapters, my brush and pen will journey from temples to tatamis, kimonos to parasols, from fountains to gardens, and modern buildings to mangas. With its myriad contrasts—cultural, temporal, and chromatic—Japan surprises and fascinates. It draws me in and, through my various encounters, grants me a giddy happiness in the shadows of its philosophy.

The time I spent with Yukie and Susumu in thoroughly modern Tokyo; my baptism into Zen practices with Aya in the heart of Kyoto traditions; my restful sojourn in Shikoku with painters Ryoichi and Tamako—the fond memory of all this will stay with me, colorful and flavorsome, simple and flamboyant. I hope one day to have the chance to float once more within this Japanese bubble.

First dream of the New Year
you are my secret
alone, I smiled

Shōu

Architectures

建築

Archi-textures

建築構造

GOLDEN PAVILION
KYOTO

Tokyo is both strikingly big and yet strikingly small—I lose my bearings as soon as I set foot upon its soil. The city stretches out to infinity, but spaces seem scaled down. Slowly, I cross the capital. The districts of Shinjuku and Asakusa are so different in architecture, yet so similar in their palettes of colors. Between modernity and tradition, I discover the many facets of Japan.

A park and cherry trees—in a leafy area, I set down my bag still caked with the dust of the Gobi and Siberia. I enter the house of Yukie and Susumu, with its sober architecture reminiscent of Bauhaus but using modern materials.

Sliding doors, smooth surfaces and wood everywhere. The air is heavy; the humidity stifling, and there is not a single breath of wind. What a joy to have an air-conditioned room surrounded by greenery!

A journey through time—Tokyo and its topicality; Kyoto and its past; Kagawa, a house where time stands still.

Pavilions spun with gold and silver, restful temples, crystal architecture—it is such a delight to be wandering the streets of Kyoto in the early morning. Never before has architecture fascinated me so with its delicacy and finesse, so fragile and pure. Noiselessly, I place my shoes next to Aya's, and glide softly over the wooden floor, in the manner of the Japanese.

Wood and paper, so simple yet so elegant, transparent tracery: I could easily spend years sitting and gazing at these temples of the past.

But I have to leave Kyoto, though I am sure to return; the town holds such fascination, as indeed does the house of Ryoichi and Tamako that I am to discover close beside Kagawa. The stuff of old storybooks, it is a traditional house with tatami mats, a house beyond my imagination and one in which I am lucky enough to stay for a few days. With its small garden, passageways, rooms that can be made bigger and smaller, futons and tatamis, I find myself living in the magic of architecture and archi-texture.

Kagawa landscapes on the island of Shikoku

The house of Ryoichi and Tamako

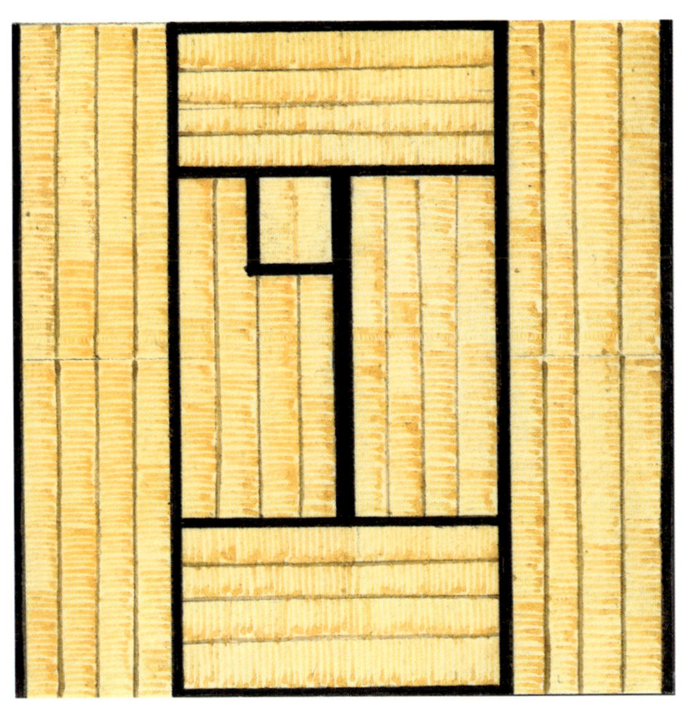

My room at Ryoichi and Tamako's house in Kagawa

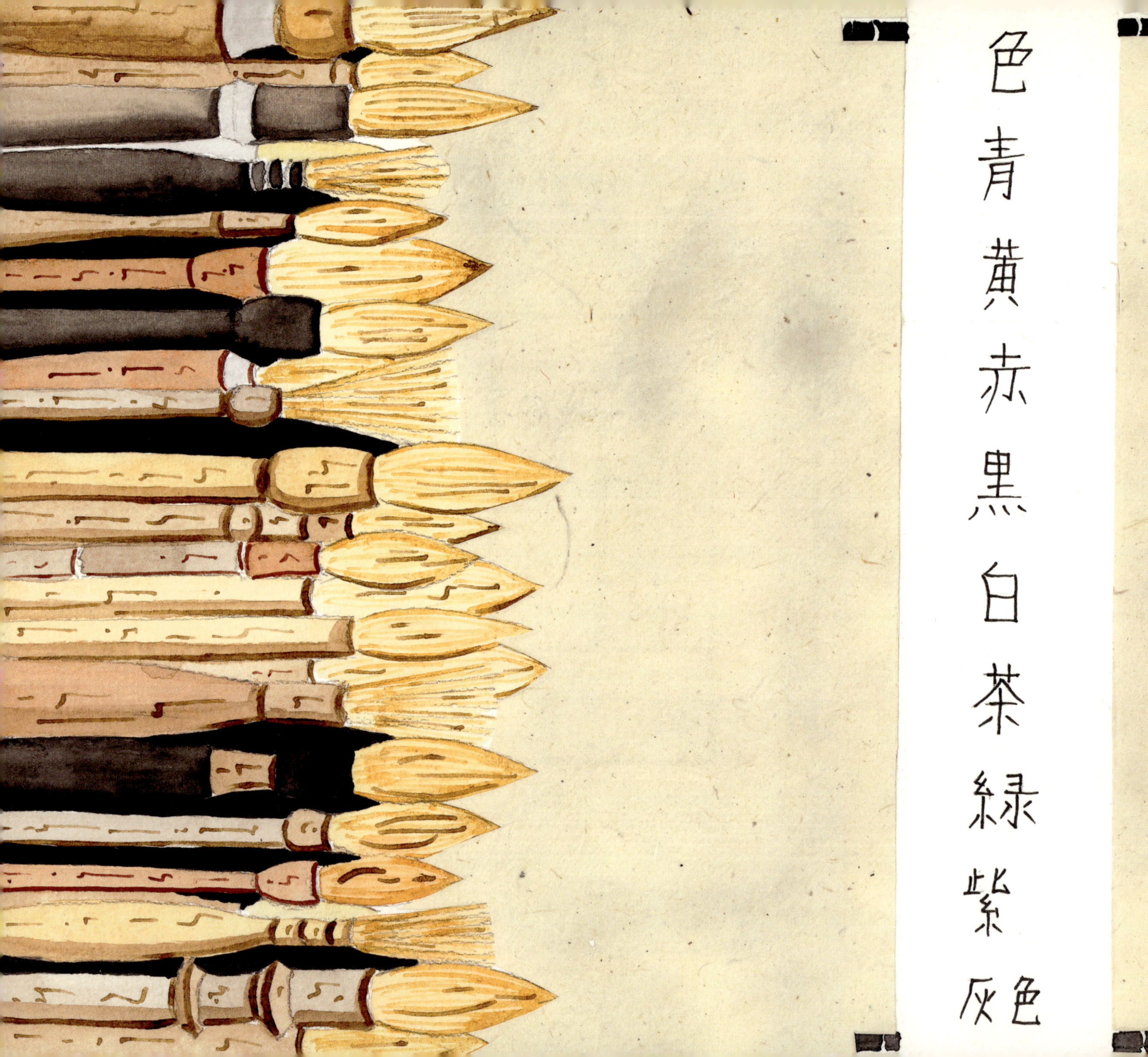
色青黄赤黒白茶緑紫灰色

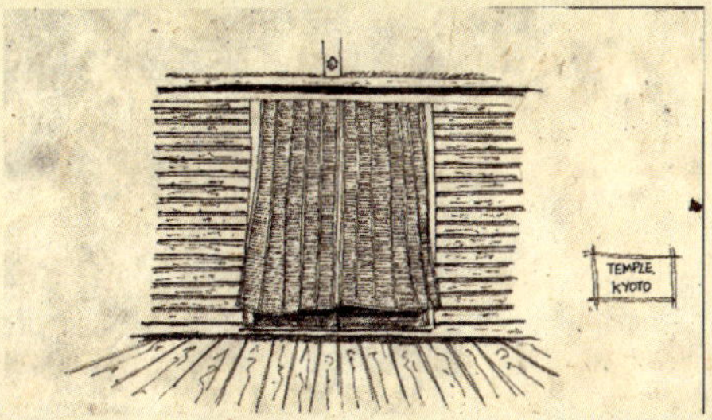

TEMPLE, KYOTO

筆

筆

ENTRANCE SENSO JI TEMPLE, KYOTO

My room by day in Gion, with its low table and chairs without legs

My room by night, with its futon placed on the tatami mats

Gates of woven bamboo at the entrance to gardens and temples

Through the ivy crawling
over the lattice door comes
evening moonlight

Bashō, "Japanese Linked Poetry"

This wall how fresh
under my tired feet
during the siesta

Bashō, "Japanese Linked Poetry"

In the candle's flame
night's splendor
frogs' croaking
Issa

Temple of Kompira-san
Dedicated to the sea and seafarers, Kompira-san is reached by climbing almost eight hundred steps that wind through lanterns and torii gateways.

The moon and I
alone are left here
cooling on the bridge

Issa, "The Haiku Seasons—Poetry of the Natural World"

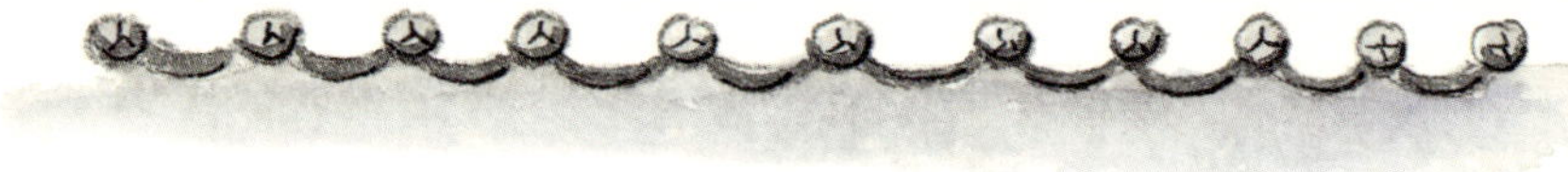

Ceramic tile patterns

Honen-in Temple in Kyoto
A drainage system that allows water to flow down a metal chain and to be collected in a stone basin.

Lanterns of various sizes are to be found in every Japanese garden, nestling under a tree. I recall the countless lanterns at Kompira-san, each more beautiful than the last.

Over the flowing water
chasing its shadow
the dragonfly

Chiyo-ni

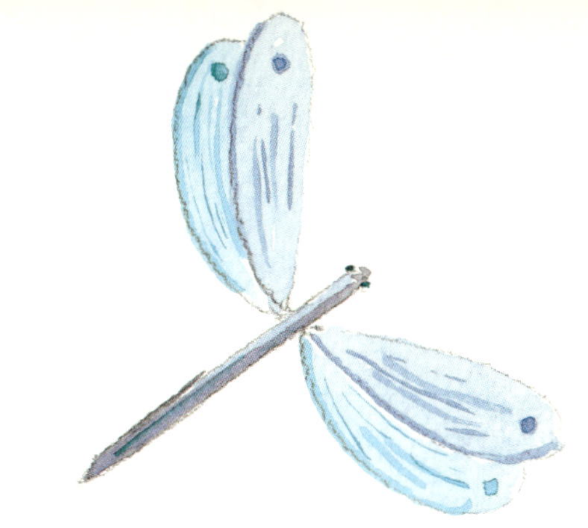

The temple of Sanjusangendo is known as the temple of a thousand goddesses. Inside, a thousand deities as tall as me are witness to the various comings and goings.

国宝三十三間堂

Yukie's "Muji" House

Customs

風習

Costumes

衣服

Geishas wearing the katsura (black wig) adorned with kanzashi (ornamental hairpins), clips, and a selection of other secret items.

One evening, Yukie shows me the kimonos belonging to her grandmother: turquoise, pink, green, dainty little flowers, a water lily, butterflies. Early next morning, I find a precious chest waiting in my room. Carefully folded for years, they are there before me—kimonos for spring and fall, each with its own season and reason. They hold so many secrets!

In the streets of Gion in Kyoto, a geisha threads her way delicately with her okobo (wooden clogs), kimono, and parasol. The sun is rising, where is she heading? She seems to have stepped straight from the pages of Arthur Golden's novel "Geisha;" a wisp of wind and she disappears around a corner.

How fascinating she is!

As time has passed, the numbers of the geishas has dwindled—how many of them are still left in the streets of Japan, the teahouses and theaters? Between modernity and tradition, the geishas drift along the seasons.

Parasols and fans—a mere detail I thought! But as soon as I set foot in Japan at the height of August, they are no mere detail: quick give me a parasol and a fan. The air is stifling! The air-conditioning at Yukie's house, the interplay of wood and paper in the sublime screens at Ryoichi's house, the mosquitoes are in their element.

One last green tea before leaving—a tea of springtime, of northern Japan, with no sugar nor milk. At every meal, at every moment of thirst, green tea is there, in its small teapot. In this blazing sun, I prefer refreshing "snow mountains"—shaved ice piled high in the colors of the rainbow.

When I happen to glimpse a geisha one morning in a street in Gion, I am back in Golden's novel once more. Which ochaya (teahouse) is she heading for? Does she play the samisen, that famous three-stringed lute? Is she a maiko (apprentice geisha) or a geiko (full-fledged geisha)? In which okiya (geisha house) does she live? Is she close to the river or the mountain? Does she have a danna (patron)?

As soon as I return to France, I will be sure to immerse myself in the fascinating universe of the geishas. So much mystery and intrigue enshroud their lives—just who are these young, beautiful women who devote their lives to tea ceremony, art, dance, music, or theater?

With their kimonos and geta or okobo, they are true tableaux vivants. In a Kyoto boutique, I am lucky enough to witness a kimono fitting. Everything is codified: there are spring kimonos, fall kimonos, for each season and every occasion a new kimono, a different obi (sash) or pocchiri (sash clasp). And then there are the hairstyles and make-up, with each geisha having her own technique, her favorite jewelry and hair clips.

From the Sea of Japan to the Western world, everyone talks about them, but what do we really know about them? Certainly not as much as we think.

Okobo

Siesta
the hand that moves
the fan stirs no more

Bashō

The butterfly
I ask to be my
traveling companion

Shiki

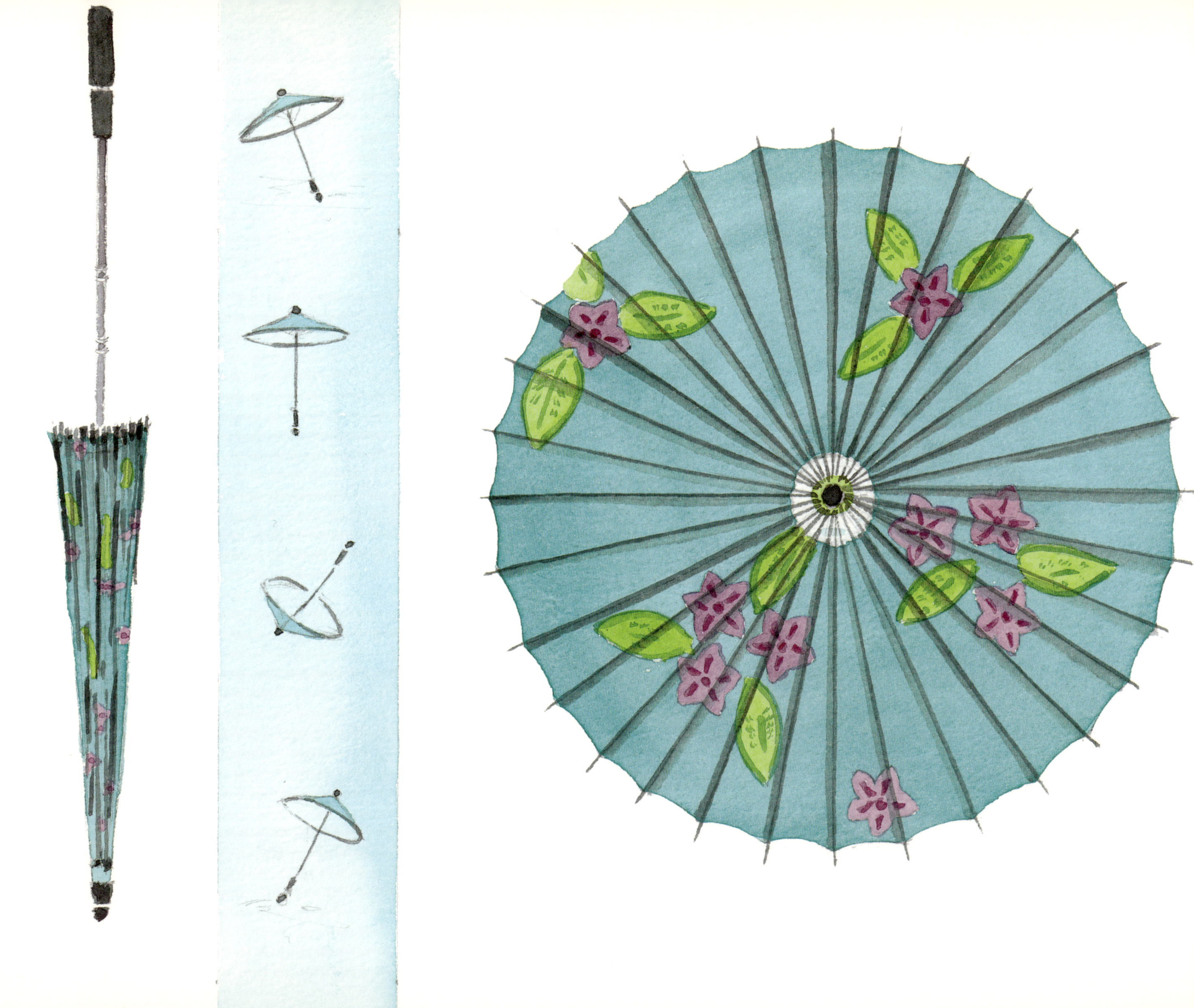

Elegant parasol, indispensable
for the skies of Japan

Man looks at the flower
the flower smiles

Zen Koan

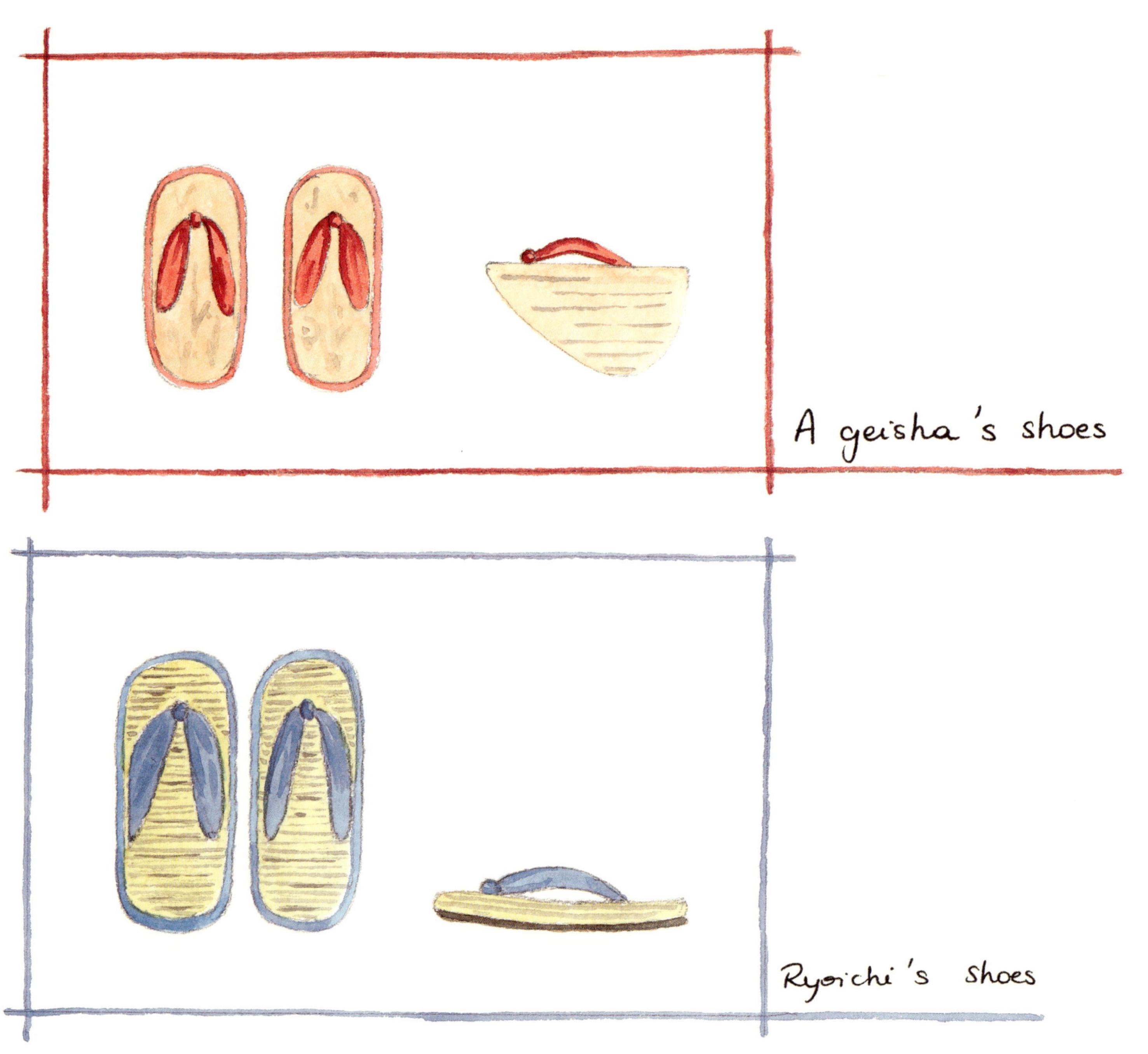
A geisha's shoes
Ryoichi's shoes

Small, cast iron, blue, black, green or ocher, the Japanese teapot awaits its green tea. Delicately set on leaves that match the teapot, the cups are steaming.

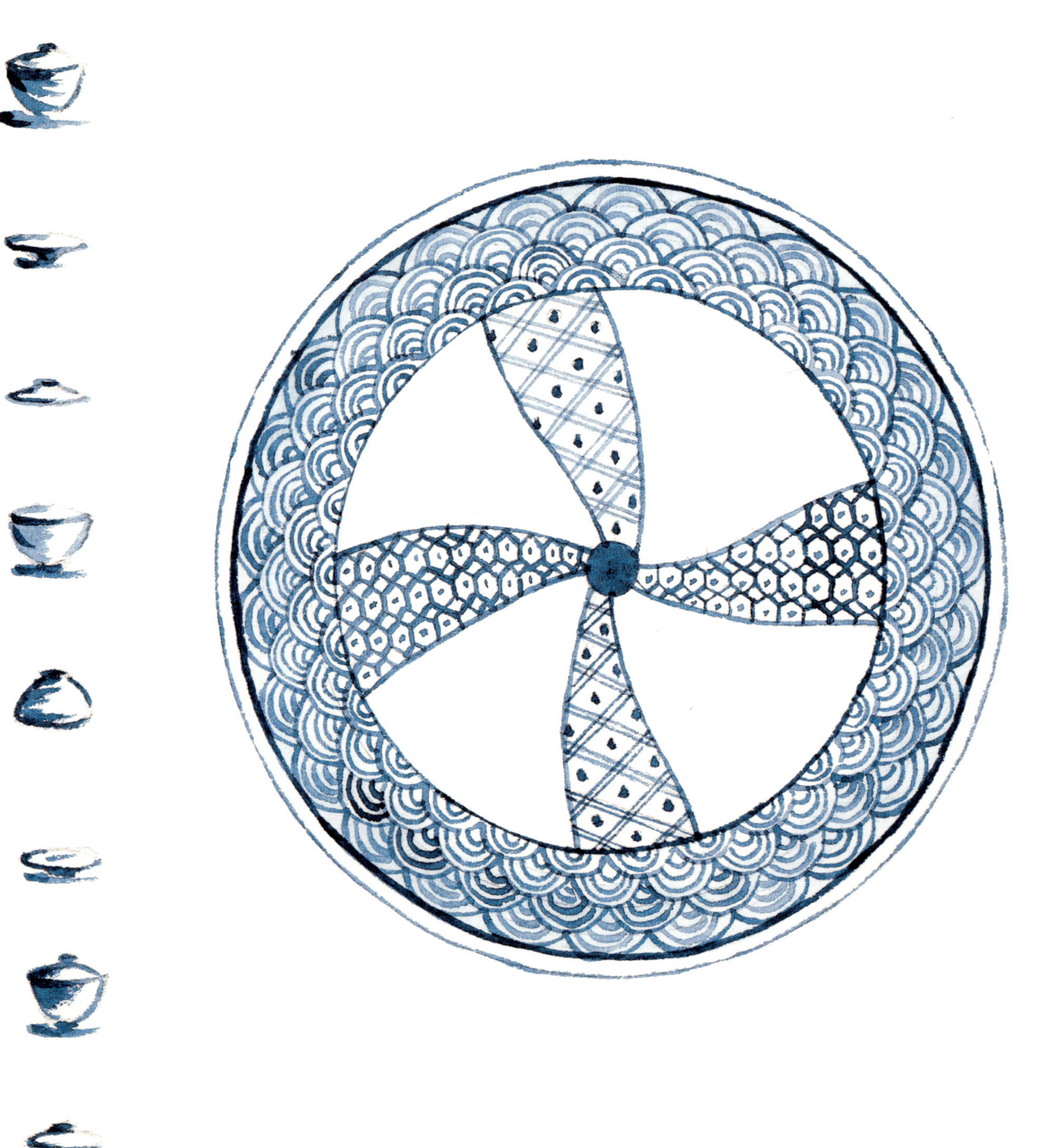

A pure marvel,
on the green, budding leaves
the light of the sun

Bashō

Secret of colors
color of a secret
streamers mingle and intermingle

Sōseki

Secret of colors
color of a secret
streamers mingle and
intermingle

Scenery

風景

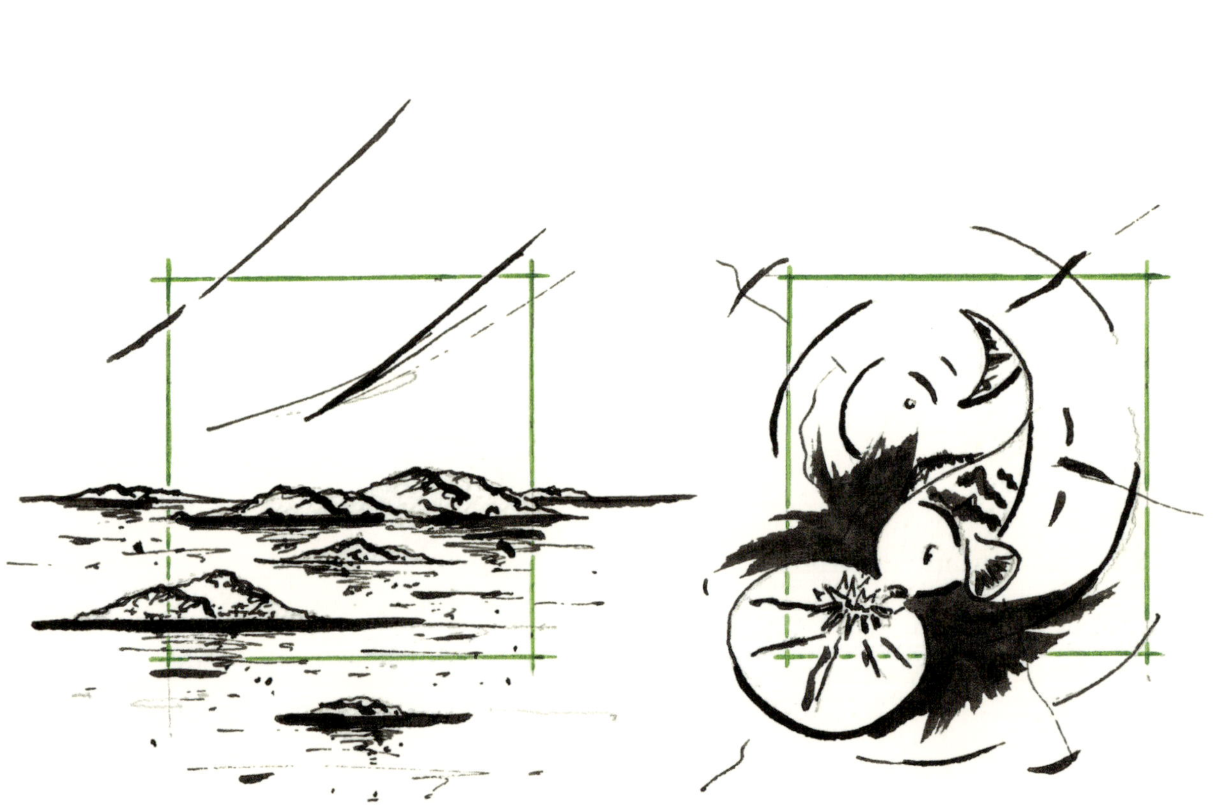

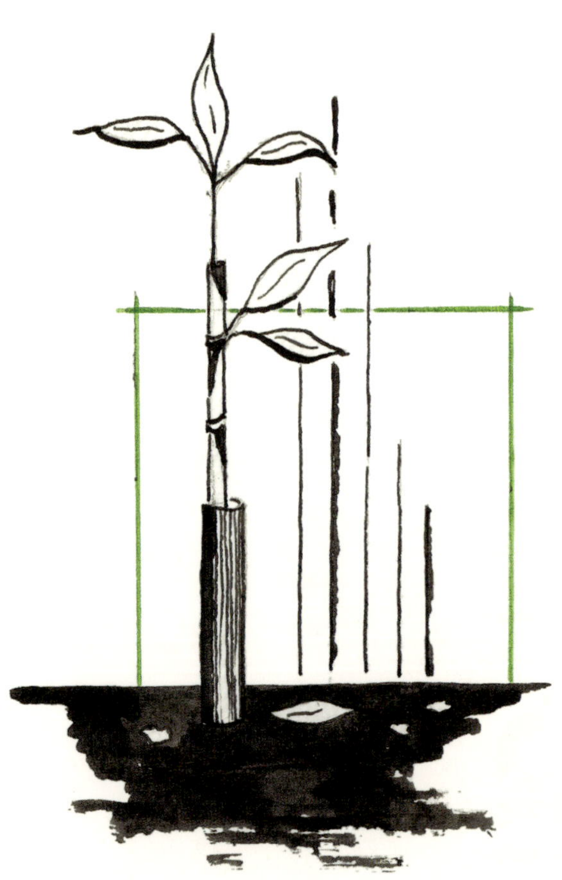

Sagacity

国禅

Three trees, small white pebbles, each morning the black cat greets me. On wakening, nature is so calm; it is hard to imagine that I am living in the heart of Tokyo. Yukie's delicate bouquet awaits me: a few roses, petals placed here and there, a large leaf. Each of her compositions is an invitation to flights of fancy. Fukie's goldfish smiles at me. My day begins west of Shinjuku, a district of Tokyo.

The scenery flashes past as the Shinkansen speeds along—rice paddies, rounded hills, and bamboo—until Kyoto slowly comes into view, huddled against the mountain.

From temple to garden and fountain to lantern, time stands still as I wander slowly along the "path of philosophy"—a stone walkway running alongside a stream filled with golden, yellow and orange carp rippling their precious hues as they follow me.

Kyoto is a beguiling town, with at every street corner something rich and strange, a wonderful garden and a wealth of refinement. From Ryoanji to Kinkakuji, it is here I would like to live.

Then there is the small train that links it to Shikoku. In the distance the islands are blue, the sea is calm, I cross majestic bridges and arrive at Kagawa, where Ryoichi and Tamako are to be my hosts.

Nature is omnipresent—wispy bamboo forests, verdant rice paddies and, behind the sliding paper screen of my room, a little Japanese garden. Lanterns, fountains, stones, and foliage tamed by Ryoichi's art and wisdom.

Evening flower
ephemeral and melancholic
tomorrow to be no more
Sōseki

Gleaming in the night
four or five bamboo
drops of moonlight

Sōseki

Which of these leaves
will be the first to fall?
Ask the wind!

Sōseki, "A History of Haiku"

A fountain in a Kyoto temple.
A leaf carefully placed beneath a stone each morning allows water to drip down into a basin. Such attention to detail and refinement!

The inland sea that I cross to reach the island of Shikoku. The light is tinged with blue and the distant islands float in a mist of indigo.

Zen garden in Kyoto: the rocks are reminiscent of small boats drifting on the sea in the shade of the mountains. Pruned and disciplined, the trees hardly dare shed their leaves on the carpet of white pebbles.

The subtle composition
of the garden at Ryoanji

Gust of wind
the leaves quiet down
Bashō

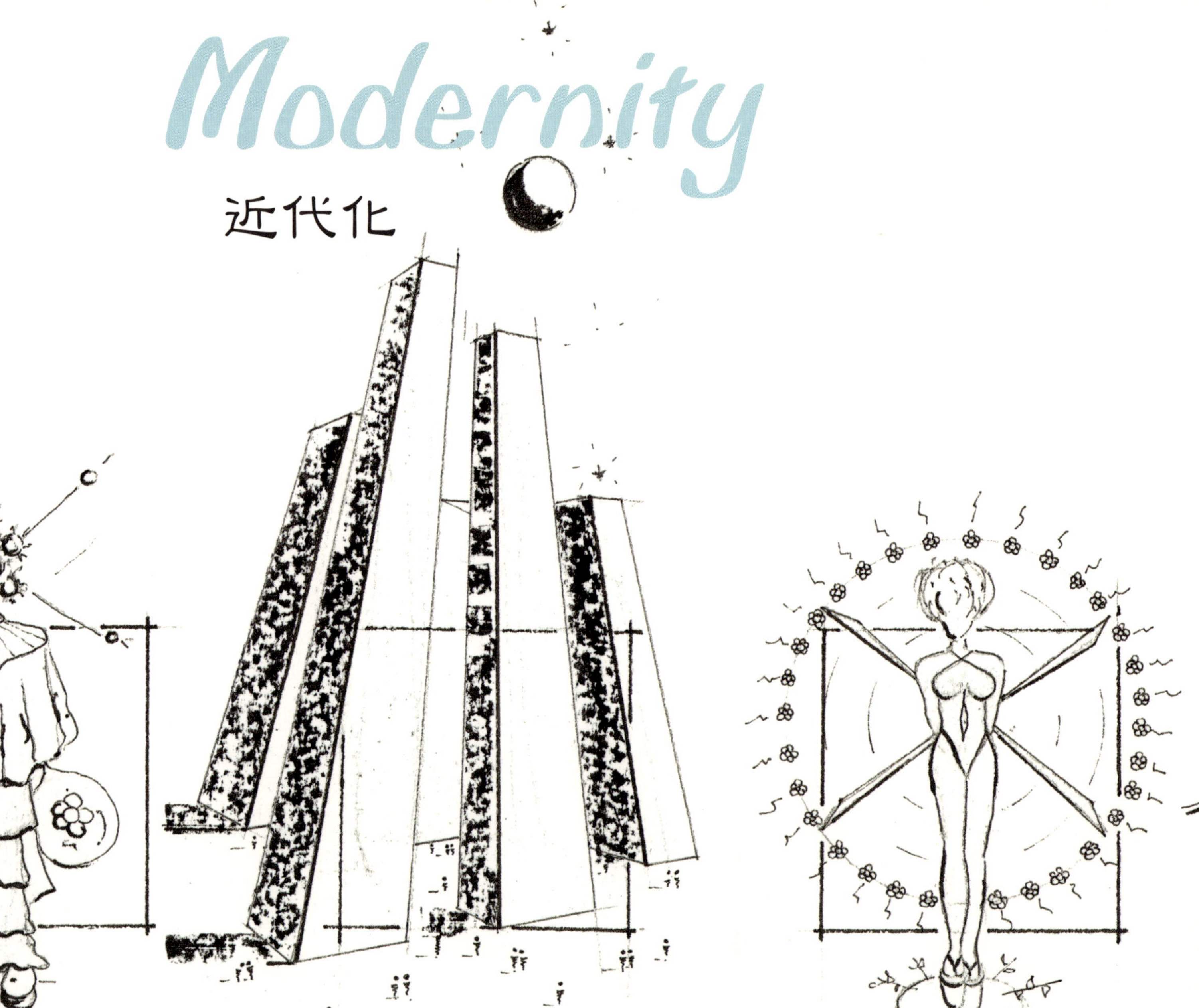
Modernity
近代化

Modern Cities

現代都市

In the land of the Rising Sun, a country of contrasts, life goes on amid temples and traditions, but also at the heart of modern buildings and the latest innovations.

Opening the door into Yukie's home, far removed from the old stone cottages of my native region of Morvan in France, I discover the universe of the prefabricated and overly-equipped house. I like Yukie's muji house, as she calls it, with its strict architecture lacking in ornament and its efficient use of space. From the bathtub that plays Chopin when it is full to the bathroom with its various multifunctional switches, I discover the delights of technology at home.

Is that sound the latest trend in music? No—it's the ring tone of a fluorescent pink mobile phone complete with silver glitter that broadcasts a flood of images and informs you that the temperature will once again reach 40°C (104°F) in the streets of Tokyo today. All the Japanese have their ears glued to these little genies of technology. "Moshi moshi?"

From conversations to consultations, between three e-mails on the latest electric-colored mobile, followed by a green tea from one of the many drink vending machines in the streets of Tokyo and a stop by the automatic photo booth that turns me into Pikachu, with blue and yellow stars and a few songs in a karaoke room, I end up in the sanctuary of Japanese youth—the bookshops devoted to manga!

Books as far as the eye can see, mile after mile of shelves, and always the same comic-strip characters—I let myself be slowly drawn into this surreal universe, so colorful and at odds with the rest. Different in format from our comic books, manga are the size of a paperback and are to be seen everywhere—in the subway, in the train, and at Yukie's house where her daughters fight over them. The manga invasion is here to stay in Japan! Farewell reality and hello to creativity, a virtual world and eternal life. Everyone, no matter what age, is caught up in the manga universe, cruising light years away from the stress around them!

Hanae, one August afternoon, underneath a tree in central Tokyo

Minae, taking a break at a sidewalk café in Asakusa

Mai, early one August morning at the Shinjuku shopping mall

Akise, August, in the sun in Ueno Park

Tatsuya, late one August afternoon in Shinjuku

Kaneo with his skateboard, sundown near Shinjuku station

Princess Miho

Encountered the first week of the year 3022 between Shinjuku and Asakusa turning to page 38 of my favorite comic. Miho, princess of the wind and colors, was getting ready to use the formidable powers of her orange ball to scale the wall of the rainbow.

Hiroe the Warrior

Intercepted in Chapter Four of "Daisies and Sword," Hiroe the Warrior was in the swamps of Shikoku, deftly wielding her weapon against the dreadful and diabolical army of daisy-eating insects.

Mayaka, the Adventuress

Glimpsed at the turn of a page on the path of the Kagawa rice paddies, Mayaka, the Adventuress, armed with her bamboo spear, was setting out to take on the Violet Mountain in her quest for immortal pollen and green tea elixir.

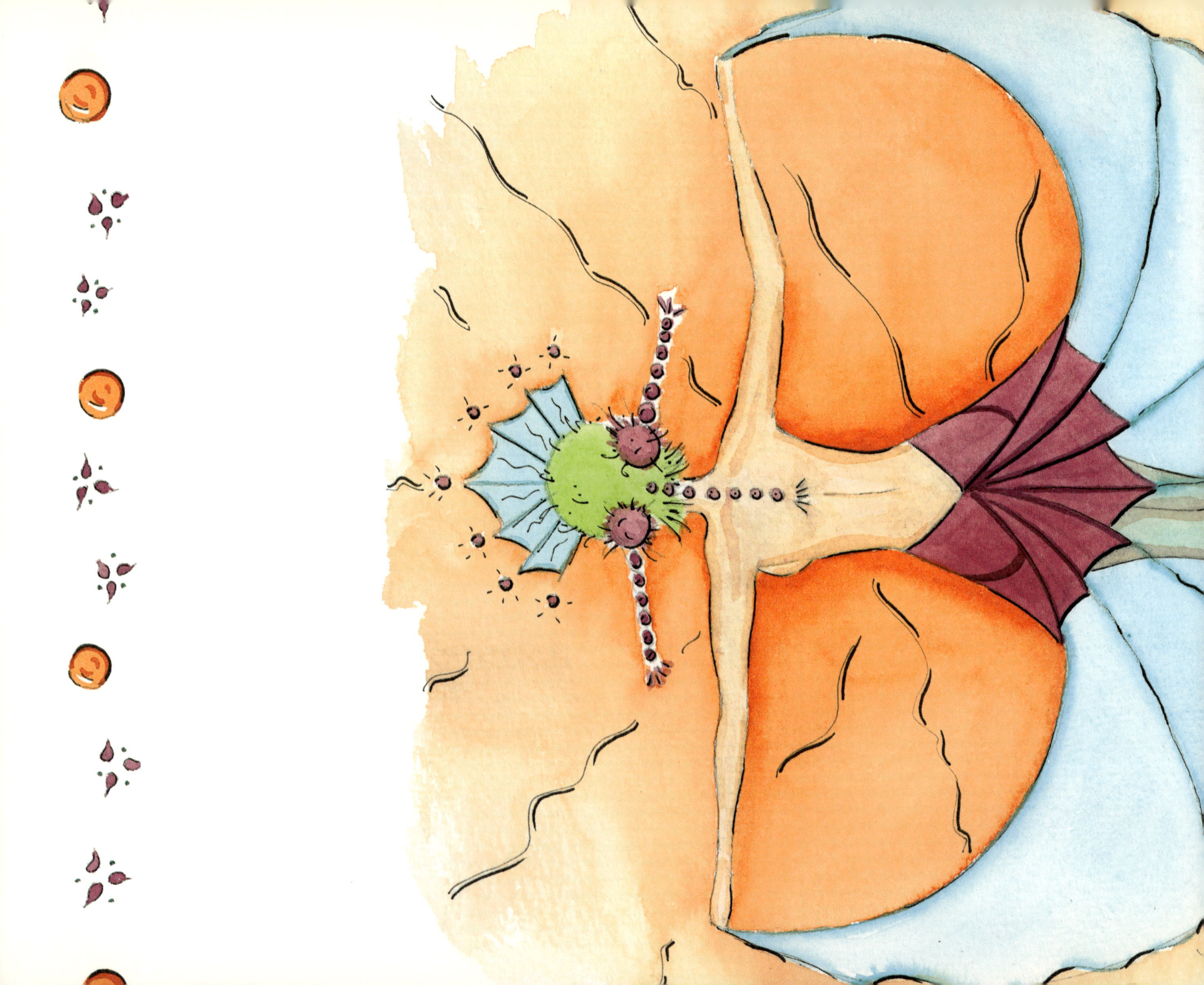

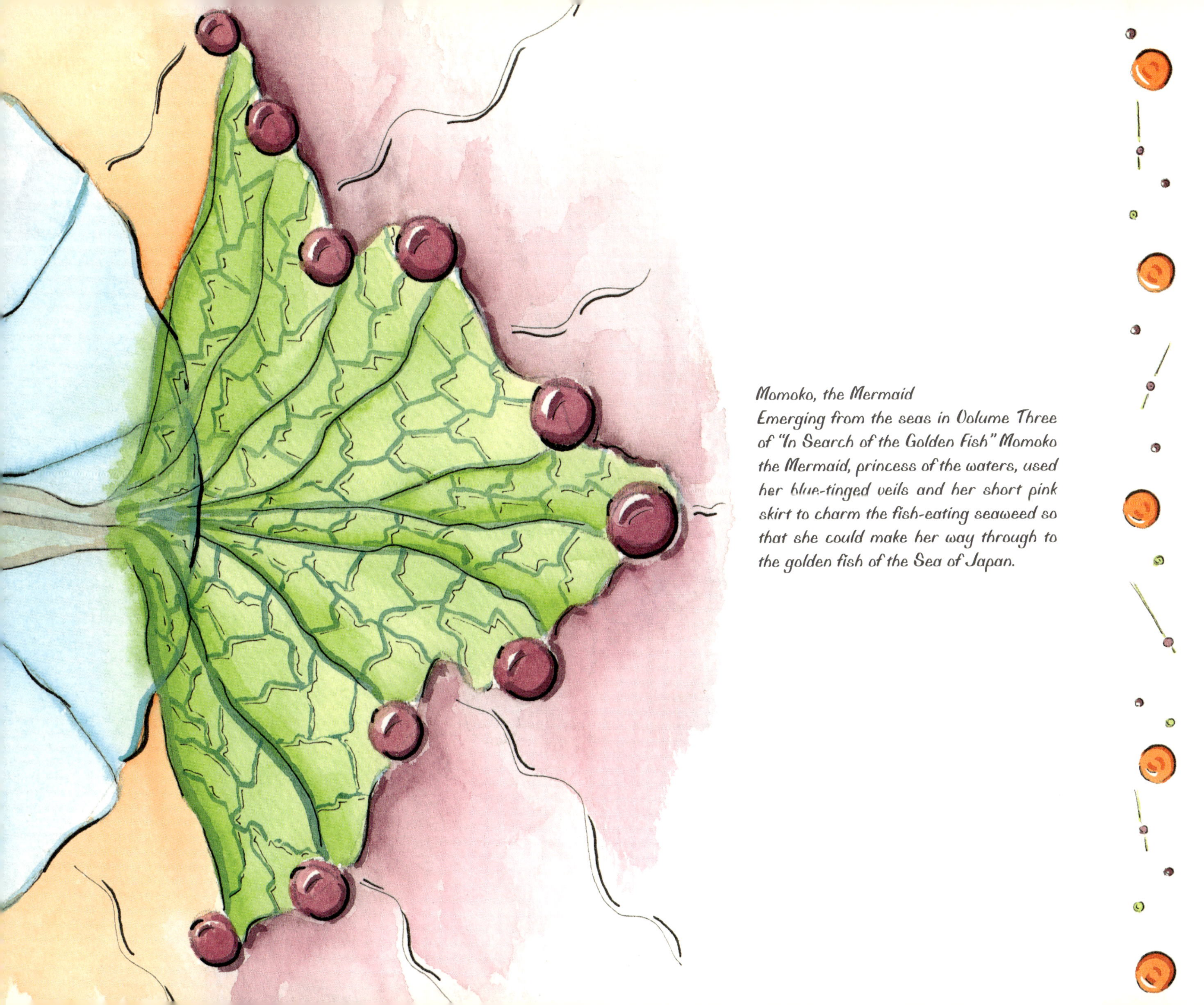

Momoko, the Mermaid
Emerging from the seas in Volume Three of "In Search of the Golden Fish" Momoko the Mermaid, princess of the waters, used her blue-tinged veils and her short pink skirt to charm the fish-eating seaweed so that she could make her way through to the golden fish of the Sea of Japan.

Tae, the Geisha

At sundown, on the heights of Gion, the beautiful young geisha Tae slipped out of her kimono to cool her body in the freshness of the stream. Golden, yellow, or orange, all the fish started blushing and goldfish were born.

Sometimes clouds form
giving respite to
moon-viewers

Bashō

Acknowledgments

A big thank you to Catherine Laulhère-Vigneau, Sandrine Balihaut-Martin, Agnès Taravella, Frédéric Hallier, and Emmanuel Laparra for their trust, valuable advice, and enthusiasm.

Thanks to Gérard Monnier and Patrick Perrin.

Many thanks to my Japanese family—my "mother," Yukie, for her patience and complicity; Susumu, Fukie and Yuka for their sessions of sketching and manga; also to their friend Sister Emiko Koïde and the sisters of the Congregation of the Infant Jesus.

Heartfelt thanks to Ryoichi and Tamako Shigeta for their welcome, their warmth, and the days spent in their wonderful house surrounded by rice paddies.

Thanks to Jean-Philippe Lenclos without whom this trip would never have existed; thanks also to Mr. Ogawa, Mr. Yoshida, and Miss Awano.

Thanks to AnnSo and Romain, Alyse, Laura, the "toutounes," Vincent, B&B, Estelle and Olive, Mathieu, Michaël, David, Isa and Marius, Lud, Isa and Timothé, Aya and Fredéric, Isa and Mike, Laurent and Céline, Gaëlle, Guillaume and Patricia, Julie, Anne-Laure and Dom, Sabine, Carine and Vincent, Juliette, Carole, Karine and Virginie, Yannick, and Aldric and Akito.

A special colorful thank you to Bérengère and her ideas.

Thanks to my parents, Ben and Belen, and to Marie-Claude, Jean-François, Réjane, my family and Samuel's, Guite, Aline and Yannick, and Bergamothe.

A colorful and contented little wink to Sandrine.

And a tremendous thank you to Samuel.